HANDBOOKS OF EUROPEAN NATIONAL DANCES

EDITED BY
VIOLET ALFORD

DANCES OF YUGOSLAVIA

Plate 1 Serbia: Belgrade region

DANCES OF YUGOSLAVIA

LJUBICA AND
DANICA JANKOVIĆ

NOVERRE PRESS

ILLUSTRATED BY
OLGA BENSON
(PLATE 3 REDRAWN BY
LUCILE ARMSTRONG)
ASSISTANT EDITOR
YVONNE MOYSE

First published in 1952
This edition published in 2021 by
The Noverre Press
Southwold House
Isington Road
Binsted
Hampshire
GU34 4PH

ISBN 978-1-914311-17-8

© 2021 The Noverre Press

CONTENTS

ᚹᚱᚾᚺ

INTRODUCTION	*Page* 7
Macedonia	8
Montenegro	9
Bosnia and Hercegovina	9
Croatia	10
Slovenia	10
Serbia	11
Dances of Ritual Origin	11
Music	14
Costume	15
A Note on Pronunciation	17
When Dancing May be Seen	18
THE DANCES	19
Poise of Body, Arm Holds	20
Characteristics of the Kolo	21
Basic Steps	22
Zupčanka	23
Zetsko Kolo	26
Tri Mlinara	30
Laka Lisa	33
BIBLIOGRAPHY	40

Illustrations in Colour, pages 2, 12, 29, 39
Map of Yugoslavia, page 6

INTRODUCTION

WE HAVE but little information concerning our dances in past times, but one early record is a fresco in the fourteenth-century monastery of Lesnovo, Macedonia, which depicts a closed circle of dancers, their arms crossed in front, and two musicians. Medieval tombstones in Bosnia portray long, solemn rows of dancers; travellers of that period speak of Kolos (Chain dances) accompanied by songs. Later both literature and folk poetry mention dances; in the nineteenth century dance-tunes began to be notated, but only in recent times has systematic research been done on our folk dances; this work—begun in Serbia in 1934—is still going on and is revealing unsuspected treasures in Yugoslavia's cultural heritage.*

The great variety of folk dances is the result of various factors, the peoples of the Federal People's Republic of Yugoslavia having lived under many different political and social conditions. South and East were mainly exposed to Turkish influences, West and North to those of the Austro-Hungarian Empire, while Dalmatia and the Adriatic

* Readers are advised to use the little map in this Handbook together with a map of Europe. Thus they will see the diversity of the frontiers of this great land, which partly accounts for the rich diversity of its dance, music and costume. Dances on the farther side of these long frontiers are shortly described in other volumes of this series: Hungary, Austria, Italy to the north and west, Rumania, Bulgaria and Greece to the east and south.—*The Editor*.

Islands were open to prolonged Italian influence. Despite this our peoples created and cultivated thousands of their own dances with much originality.

MACEDONIA

Always a region of conflict, Macedonia remained under Turkish rule until the Balkan War of 1912. Amongst its original elements her choreography contains remnants of Turkish dances, and some oriental influences have been assimilated. Complex rhythms, syncopated steps are characteristic and can be seen in the fascinating Teškoto, the grave Kolo type belonging to Lazaropolje, in various Lisas in the Skoplje region, and in many others.

The Lesnoto, the light Kolo type, comprises hundreds of dances to various tunes, the style varying according to costumes, occupations and economic conditions. For instance people from formerly backward regions, who had to leave their homes to seek work elsewhere, use the *pečalbari* style, heavy and expressive of homesickness, until in the urge to dance they gradually shake it off, working up to a joyful climax; while in contrast the peasant farmers, who know nothing of this nostalgia, pass more quickly into gaiety. The Skoplje region excels in this high-spirited, almost flighty manner of dancing. Around Kičevo the *čifčije*, workers on the one-time feudal estates, have a style recalling past obligatory subservience to Turkish masters. But the clenched fist held behind his back by the Kolo leader was symbolic of the ever-present resistance, and since the expulsion of the Turkish masters the people of Kičevo have held themselves ever more and more erect in the dance.

Macedonia, a country where old men who are highly skilled dancers are to be found, shows a considerable difference in the styles of the two sexes, men dancing with far less restraint than the women. The most general dance form is the open Kolo, the leader of which may perform solo steps.

MONTENEGRO

Encircled by their high mountains, the Montenegrins, of all our peoples, best preserved their native land from foreign domination. Their chivalrous spirit is reflected in their free, high leaps—as though an unseen lever precipitated them into the air. This free style excels itself in the Couple dance called Po crnogorski ('A la Monténégrine'), without music of any sort, and in Skoke, during which onlookers urge them in song to hold out as long as possible. Their Kolos, too, demonstrate their brave spirit. In these the sexes are divided, the women dancing with restraint, repeating what the men have just sung. Crmničko Kolo is lively, the dancers crossing their arms behind their backs; in Tanac dancers weave in and out. All are sung or danced to the thudding of the feet only. Instrumental music is not used in Montenegrin dancing.

The Kolo of the Boka Kotorska merchant navy is a solemn dance opening the St. Trifun festivities in Kotor.

BOSNIA AND HERCEGOVINA

These peoples, who have lived first under Turkish and then under Austrian rule, often danced without any musical accompaniment whatever, and this characteristic continues today. Such 'music-less' dancing, dependent on rhythm alone, can nevertheless rise to the heights of ecstasy. Wonderful it is to witness and wonderful to hear, the thud of twenty or thirty pairs of feet in precise unison working upon the senses as much as, or probably more than, the most exciting tune.

Other Kolos, such as the Trusa, may be performed in this remarkable way or to music. Round Ljubuški the 'Darling Kolo', Dilber, is a favourite, while a Couple dance, Lindjo, found near Neum Klek, is very temperamental in style. Indeed these sons of rough and mountainous

Hercegovina, accustomed to big strides as they step from one rock to another, are apt to become highly exhilarated after a quiet beginning to the dance. In Bosnia the Kolo of Sarajevo is widespread, while the Old Bosnian Kolo has several variants.

CROATIA

This province was under the rule of Austria-Hungary until 1918. It is here, in the environs of the town of Zagreb, that we come across the curious shivering or vibration of the whole body, as though some giant hand were shaking the dancers. This strange characteristic has given rise to such dance names as The Shaking and The Old Sieve, while on the coast and Adriatic islands ancient ceremonial dances have been preserved: for instance in Istria the Balun, on the island of Krk the Tanac, on Korčula Sword dances, the Kumpanija (the Company) and the famous Moresca,* which is a dance-drama depicting a struggle between Moors and Turks—a local deviation from the usual Christian-versus-Moor tradition—over a Moslem girl.

In Slavonia we note that dance verses, sometimes improvised, are sung and that style and dance technique seem to express the carefree disposition of these people and their ardent temperament.

SLOVENIA

This country, long under Austrian domination, shows as a natural result a strong liking for the Pair dance. Some Kolos are combined with Couple dancing, but the latter is the most frequent. We find the Polka for instance, particularly at weddings, while in the Bela (White) Krajina region there are open, snake-like Kolos, closed Kolos and interesting dances of ritual origin. Research work and restoration of Slovene dances are in progress.

* See *Dances of Italy* in this series.—*Editor.*

SERBIA

Serbia freed her central regions from Turkish rule in the beginning of the nineteenth century, and in these regions the Chain dance predominates together with the straight-line dance, dancers tightly grasping their neighbours' belts on either side, their arms crossed. The Sestorka is a humorous dance; the Vlahinja type is widely spread, its name derived from the Turkish way of denoting the Serbs —Vlachs. Formerly this was the dance performed by brides as they bade farewell to their old homes. Before her wedding a girl had to lead the Kolo three times round the house, bowing each time she passed the door. Curious Turks used to gather to watch this traditional farewell of the Vlahinja, the Serbian maiden, and the name passed from the girl to the dance itself.

Serbia is rich in types and steps. Every region has its own dance style; in the Morava valley it is easy and light, in the Kolubara region soft, in the Vlasina area vigorous, but everywhere the style is gay and high-spirited. In Kosovo, which remained under the Turks till 1912, the towns had assimilated oriental characteristics while the villages retained more of their native temperament. In Prizren, Kolos and the curious and unusual Kalač have retained the charm of the dignified Serbian style of that town; while in the northern part, Vojvodina, freed from Austro-Hungarian rule in 1918, Couple dances are not infrequent. A dance in groups of three, each young man having a girl on either side, is one of the most intricate Vojvodina dances.

DANCES OF RITUAL ORIGIN

Besides the ceremonial Moresca and Sword dances already mentioned, we find in some dances survivals of magic dating from before our era. These are now rapidly disappearing.

Plate 2 Croatia: Sisak region

Of old the end of harvesting in the Bačka was celebrated by a procession, the leader of the harvesters wearing a crown made of ears of corn, and by a Kolo during which the dancers poured water on each other—to ensure rain for the next sowing. The Dodole, amongst our most interesting survivals, again invoking rain and consequent fertility, were formerly performed when there was a drought. A group of young girls would go dancing from house to house, singing as they went songs which contained elements of prayers for rain. One of them, the Dodola herself, naked beneath leaves, flowers and green grass—a feminine Jack-in-the-Green—performed alone. The householder would come running out with jars and souse her with water, which imitative magic would assuredly bring rain.

The Lazarice, Spring dances combined with song, performed by women on St. Lazarus' Day, eight days before Easter, have lately been taken over by Gypsy women who dance for money, while the Kraljice (Queens) appear on St. George's Day or at Whitsuntide. Their tall, mitre-like head-dresses, often adorned with a sacred picture, make a wonderful show; they carried swords but later handkerchiefs and fluttering bannerets of red silk or roughly woven cloth, decorated with apples, bells and magic plants. Their aim, like that of the Lazarice, is to 'bring in' health and happiness.

Kolos also may sometimes have a ritual significance as those performed with banners at weddings, which are supposed to protect the newly married couple from evil spirits. There is, for example, the dance called 'Lead the Kolo, Bojana', performed for this purpose; others also to accompany the dressing and shaving of the bridegroom, while others, such as Šareno Kolo, are designed to bring the young couple together and generally end wedding festivities. Ritual Kolos are done at Whitsuntide and on Easter Monday and round the Midsummer fire.

But our most remarkable ritual dances are perhaps the

Rusalia of Macedonia. Men dancers come out between Christmas and the Epiphany with wooden swords, attired in ritual dance costume and with ritual gear. Their impressive 'slow-motion' actions and steps are to invoke health and healing and a good harvest next autumn. In their white costumes with little skirts and their measured sword-movements—each to himself, spaced so far apart as to almost constitute a solo for each man; not to be confused with the well known European Hilt-and-Point dance—they make a never-to-be-forgotten picture of a present-day dance of one-time magical intent.

Danced at other seasons and in ordinary garb, these dances are not of a ritual nature.

MUSIC

Our varied populations have produced many sorts of instruments for accompanying our dances. In Serbia we have bagpipes and the *duduk*, a shepherd's flute; in Macedonia the *šupeljka*, a primitive flute, and the *zurla* which is a primitive oboe; percussion is represented by the bass drum, called *goč*, in Serbia, and the large drum called *tupan* in Macedonia. Croatia owns bagpipes called *mešnica*, the peasant wind instrument known as *sopele* and many others, but the mandoline-like *tamburica* is being used more and more.

Bosnia and Hercegovina share some of these, and have bagpipes of their own.

Certain towns own a whole popular orchestra, *čalgije*, but true folk instruments are slowly disappearing and the violin, the accordion and brass are creeping in. Women (more often than men) like to dance to song accompaniments and sometimes without any music at all, accompanied only by the sound of their feet and the jingling of the gold coins with which they are adorned. In the greater part of the country the dancing follows the music, but in

Macedonia and Southern Serbia the music follows the dancing.

Dance tunes may be ritual or secular. In the South the ritual tunes are archaic and sung slowly and solemnly. Some tunes are bitonal or even semitonal in compass, producing a peculiar trilling, while others have a wide compass and are in fact elaborate; at the beginning or the end —sometimes in the middle—comes the strange cry or rather sigh, the *ikanje.* This archaic 'Eee—e—e—e', on no determined note, carries one back to some far distant past, and exciting it is in its stirring of folk memory. We know the usual 2/4, 3/4 and 4/4 rhythms but also 5/4, while in Macedonia and Serbia polyrhythmic combinations such as 4/8 + 5/8; 7/8 + 4/8; 9/8 + 11/8 and others are not at all rare.

Sometimes the length of melodic and dance phrase does not coincide; they overlap each other, synchronising and again diverging. This in practice is very effective and by no means disturbs the dance steps, as the dancers continue their rhythm during the odd bars until the melody is caught up again.

COSTUME

Geographical conditions and the occupations of the wearers are largely responsible for shape, material and even colour in our enormously rich and varied heritage of costume.

In the Macedonian mountains the warm and heavy costumes are in harmony with both the climate and the grave style of dancing. In the agricultural and very warm area near Skoplje the light clothes are in keeping with the airy manner of dancing. The women's dress is either white with black embroidery and a red apron (Skopska Crna Gora) or very colourful (Blatija; see Plate 4). Men have a broad red belt, red waistcoat and closely gathered shirt which spreads out when the dancers twist and turn.

Macedonia offers an inexhaustible source of decorative costumes and geometrical designs.

Montenegrin men wear blue trousers and a red upper garment with gold embroidery. Pastel colours are characteristic of the women's dress, and the cut of the garments shows off the figure beautifully as the women dance sedately (see Plate 3).

In Bosnia and Hercegovina the main feature of the women's dress is a *zubun* (upper part of their costume). Bosnian embroidery is dark or red, mostly in geometric designs; men wear worsteds and jerkins. In Hercegovina the embroidery is multicoloured, mostly red with floral designs; men don broadcloth and gold embroidery much like the Montenegrins.

The *zubun* is also worn in the Croatian regions near the Bosnian Krajina. The villages round Zagreb offer a variegated exhibition of women's attire. The vicinity of Sisak boasts finely ornamented women's dresses (see Plate 2). Red colour and floral motifs predominate in the Croatian costumes.

In Slovenia the Bela Krajina (White Krajina) is thus called from the white costumes. Girls have white kerchiefs on their heads with stiff uplifted corners so that when they dance white doves with wings stretched out seem to be resting on their heads. The mountaineers wear warm, colourful clothes.

In central Serbia, Šumadija, pleated woollen skirts with multi-coloured intersecting stripes and velvet vests embroidered in gold are worn. Men have woollen worsted or broadcloth embellished with silk braid. In the Posavina region we see women wearing vertically striped multi-coloured skirts, open in front and tucked in at the sides of the belt (see Plate 1) to show the embroidered chemise. In the Vojvodina, the Serbian costume has disappeared, but in Kosovo and Metohija it still lives, showing elaborate embroidery and small ornaments.

Various kinds of leather moccasins and gaily ornamented stockings complete the picture.

Folk costumes inevitably undergo modifications, and in some localities have now become only museum pieces. But the planned work for the promotion of festivals throughout our country has brought to light the valuable material we possess, not only in folk dance and folk music but in our regional costumes also.

A NOTE ON PRONUNCIATION

The main language of Yugoslavia is Serbo-Croat, which is written by the Serbs in Cyrillic characters while the Croats use the Roman alphabet. Croat spellings are used in this book.

A is pronounced as in 'f*a*ther'; E as in 'm*e*n'; I as in 'pol*i*ce'; O as in 'm*o*re'; U as in 'r*u*le'.

C is like the TS in 'bi*ts*'. It is never pronounced K.

Č is the English CH in '*ch*at'.

Ć as in 'be*t y*ou', or in the old-fashioned pronunciation of 'na*t*ure' (*nay-tyoor*, not *nay-tcher*).

G is always hard as in '*g*et'.

J is the English Y as in '*y*es'.

S is always unvoiced as in '*s*it'.

Š is pronounced as the English SH.

Ž has the sound of the s in 'plea*s*ure'.

The other letters have roughly the same sound-values as in English. Note that R can take the place of a vowel: to pronounce the name of the island of Krk, say the Scottish 'kirk' with a well-trilled R and keeping the vowel as short as you can.

OCCASIONS WHEN DANCING MAY BE SEEN

St. Lazarus' Day (*8 days before Easter*)	Lazarice: girls' Spring songs and dances.
St. George's Day (*May 6th*) *and Whitsuntide*	Kraljice (Queens): girls' Spring songs and dances at Vlasotinci and Subotica.
Easter Monday	Metliško Kolo (in Slovenia).
Whitsuntide	Črnomelj Kolo-Most in the White Krajina (Slovenia).
St. John's Eve (*June 23rd*)	Dancing round bonfires in many parts of the country.
End of Harvest	Dancing in the Bačka (Vojvodina) and in the vicinty of Lazarevac (Serbia).
Between Christmas and Epiphany	Rusalia dances in Macedonia (neighbourhood of Djevdjelija).

Also at *sabors* (local solemn gatherings), weddings, on Sundays and on the completion of field work; while preparing feathers for pillows or taking corn off the cob; and now at numerous more modern gatherings of young people.

THE DANCES

TECHNICAL EDITORS
MURIEL WEBSTER AND KATHLEEN P. TUCK

ABBREVIATIONS
USED IN DESCRIPTION OF STEPS AND DANCES

r—right ⎫ referring to R—right ⎫ describing turns or
l—left ⎭ hand, foot, etc. L—left ⎭ ground pattern
C—clockwise C-C—counter-clockwise

For descriptions of foot positions and explanations of any ballet terms the following books are suggested for reference:

A Primer of Classical Ballet (Cecchetti method). Cyril Beaumont.

First Steps (R.A.D.). Ruth French and Felix Demery.

The Ballet Lover's Pocket Book. Kay Ambrose.

Reference books for description of figures:

The Scottish Country Dance Society's Publications. Many volumes, from Thornhill, Cairnmuir Road, Edinburgh 12.

The English Folk Dance and Song Society's Publications. Cecil Sharp House, 2 Regent's Park Road, London N.W.1.

The Country Dance Book I–VI. Cecil J. Sharp. Novello & Co., London.

POISE OF BODY

The poise is upright and proudly held by the men. The knees are bent softly and are never held stiff or straight, either when bearing the weight of the body or when raised in the air. In the slow Kolos the legs may be raised quite high. The movements of the women are more restrained, especially in some of the dances. The women never raise their knees as high as the men in any step. Vibration, when used, is literally a shaking of the whole body from head to foot and is not done to musical beats. The characteristic feature of the dances is the dynamic force which emanates from each dancer and which is expressed in the whole bearing of the men.

ARM HOLDS

These vary in the different Kolos and are described under the names of the Kolos concerned:

Tri Mlinara

Closed Kolo or circle of dancers in which all hands are joined. The men and women stand alternately and join hands firmly, with arms very slightly bent.

Župčanka

Open Kolo or semicircle. Men and women stand alternately, the women placing their fingers lightly in the palms of the men's hands from above.

Zetsko Kolo

(a) One closed Kolo. (b) Two closed Kolos—one inside the other. In both these, women form one-half of circle, men the other half. (c) Double Kolo (men only), in which dancers in the lower circle cross hands behind their backs and then grasp hands of man on each side. Dancers in the upper circle, standing on the shoulders of the lower circle, place hands on shoulders of man on each side.

Laka Lisa

The dancers are connected in chains by strings of coloured beads, kerchiefs or small towels. In some of the Macedonian dances the dancers hold each other by the belt of the man on either side. When an ordinary hand-grasp is used the hands are held firmly but rather low, with arms straight.

CHARACTERISTICS OF THE KOLO

The Kolo is always led by one dancer, generally a man. This leader is the first dancer of an open Kolo. He stands at the right of the chain of dancers if the Kolo moves first to the right, and at the left if it moves first to the left. The Kolo may start with a single dancer—the leader—and be joined by the other dancers in turn. Dancers may drop out when they tire and their places may be taken by other dancers. The Kolo usually has many phases and very often works up from a gentle swaying motion to more animated movement, which dies down to a moderate level according to the directions of the musician and the Kolo leader.

BASIC STEPS

The steps themselves are simple, the interest lying in the rhythm. Dancers may improvise on the basic steps, especially the leader, who adds leaps and turns at will and then picks up the basic steps with the other dancers. These steps consist of walking, running and hopping, with the following varieties of crossing and closing steps done to varied timing, as is later described.

Crossing Step

(*a*) FRONT CROSS. One foot is crossed in front of the other and weight is transferred, the dancer moving sideways to R or L. The shoulders are usually held square to the front unless otherwise indicated.

(*b*) BACK CROSS. One foot is crossed behind the other, the dancer moving sideways as described in Front Cross.

Closing Step

One foot is brought rather quickly beside the other, very often on an '*and*' off-beat. This closed position is usually held for one or more beats.

ŽUPČANKA

Region   Serbia. Plate 1.

Character   Gay and lively, for both men and women. The body is vibrated slightly, especially on Closing step, and the knees are bent softly throughout.

Formation   An Open Kolo—men and women standing alternately in a wide semicircle, grasping hands as described under Arm Holds. The leader may guide the Kolo into spiral patterns (Diagrams A and B), the dancers travelling more to the right than to the left so that progress is made. (O = woman, □ = man.)

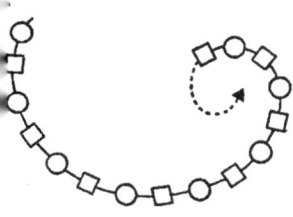 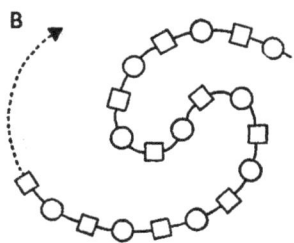

Dance
Dancers face slightly to R when moving to R, and to L when moving to L.

Step to R on r foot [*beat 1*].
Hop on r foot [*and*].
Cross l foot in front of r foot [*beat 2*].
Hop on l foot [*and*].

MUSIC
Bars

1

ZUPČANKA

Serbia: Noted by Vladimir R. Djordjević
Arranged by Arnold Foster

Step to R on r foot [*beat 1*]. Close l foot to r foot, not changing weight [*and*]. Hold the closed position [*beat 2*].	2
Repeat, moving to L and beginning with l foot.	3–4
Step on r foot, placing it obliquely forward in front of l foot, at the same time raising l foot just off ground [*beat 1*]. Step on l foot in place, raising r foot just off ground [*and*]. Close r foot to l foot [*beat 2*]. Hop on r foot, raising l foot [*and*].	5
Repeat, beginning with l foot and placing it obliquely forward in front of r foot.	6
Repeat the whole sequence as often as desired.	

N.B.—Music and dance phrases do not coincide in length, but the dance continues regardless of this until melody and movement again synchronise.

ZETSKO KOLO

Region Montenegro (Plate 3); Hercegovina: Gacko.

Character Solemn and sedate, the women more restrained than the men. Danced to the accompaniment of unison singing. Each verse is sung first by the men, then repeated by the women.

Formation Varies in the regions: (1) Montenegro—Closed Kolo or two Closed Kolos (Diagrams A and B). (2) In Hercegovina (Gacko)—Double Kolo; men only, one Kolo on the shoulders of another, further described under Arm Holds, p. 20. Only the lower circle of dancers performs the steps.

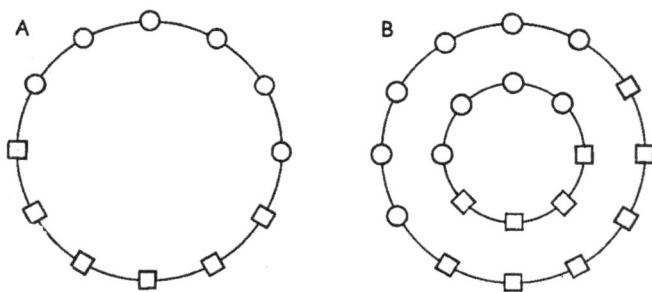

Dance	MUSIC Bars
All place hands on the shoulders of the next dancers in Closed Kolo.	
Step to R on r foot [*beat 1*].	1

ZETSKO KOLO

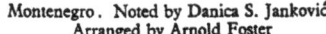
Montenegro. Noted by Danica S. Janković
Arranged by Arnold Foster

1. *Kolo, kolo, let us join hands,*
   Kolo, kolo, let us join hands.

2. *Grasp your white hands in the kolo,*
   Grasp your white hands in the kolo.

3. *Spring upon your feet so lightly,*
   Spring upon your feet so lightly.

4. *Happiness will be yours rightly,*
   Happiness will be yours rightly.

Cross l foot in front of r foot, changing weight and moving to R [*beat 2*].

Step to R on r foot, shooting l leg obliquely forward to R, men's feet in the air, those of the women on the ground [*beat 1*].
Hold this position [*beat 2*].

2

Bring l foot to r foot, shooting r leg obliquely backward to L, men's feet in the air, those of the women on the ground [*beat 1*].
Hold this position [*beat 2*].

3

Repeat the whole sequence as often as desired.

N.B.—Music and dance phrases do not coincide in length, but the dance continues regardless of this until melody and movement again synchronise.

Plate 3   Montenegro

TRI MLINARA

(*The Three Millers*)

Region   Croatia: Sisak region. Plate 2.

Character   Gay and lively; the small Closing step is slightly accented and is accompanied by a vibration of the whole body.

Formation   A Closed Kolo at first (Diagram A), breaking up into couples on Steps 4 and 5 (Diagram B).

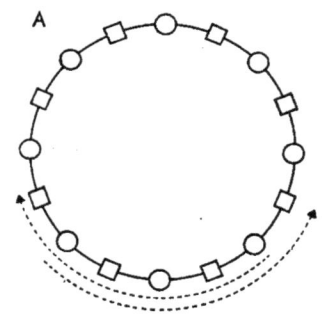

Dance	MUSIC
Men and women stand alternately, grasping hands.	*Bars*
1 Step to L on l foot [*beat 1*].	1
Close r foot to l foot, changing weight [*beat 2*].	
Step to L on l foot [*beat 1*].	2

TRI MLINARA

Croatia: Sisak region
Noted by Danica S. Janković
Arranged by Arnold Foster

Close r foot to l foot without changing weight [*and*].	
Hold the closed position [*beat 2*].	
Repeat, moving to R, beginning with r foot.	3–4
During this step the Kolo contracts.	
Step forward on l foot [*beat 1*].	5
Close r foot to l foot, changing weight [*beat 2*].	
Repeat twice.	6–7

Step forward on l foot [*beat 1*].
Close r foot to l foot without changing weight [*and*].
Hold the closed position [*beat 2*].

3 During this step the Kolo expands.
Repeat movements of Step 2, travelling backward with r foot, to finish in twos (Diagram B). | 9–12

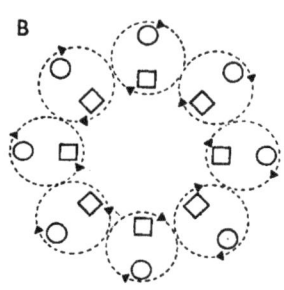

4 Partners change places, moving C with 6 running steps, beginning with l foot. | 5–7
Step forward on l foot [*beat 1*]. | 8
Close r foot to l foot without changing weight [*and*].
Hold the closed position [*beat 2*].

5 Repeat, moving C to own places, beginning with r foot. | 9–12

Repeat the whole dance as often as desired.

LAKA LISA

✳✳✳✳✳✳

Region Macedonia: Skoplje region. Plate 4.

Character The women are restrained and dignified, the men lively and sometimes acrobatic. The rhythm of the dance (♩ ♫) is in contrast to the rhythm of the tune (♫ ♩) in the most characteristic parts.

Formation Varied, and best described under diagrams. The numbers of men and women need not be equal.

DIAGRAM A

Open Kolo, men in the right-hand half and women in the left. The dancers hold each other by cords or coloured beads, or by the ends of handkerchiefs. The Kolo leader

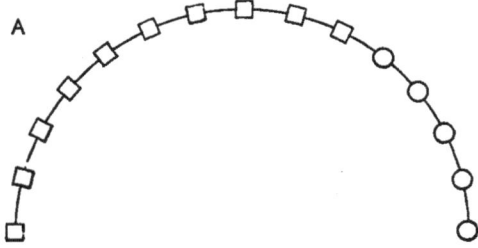

from time to time swings his beads or handkerchief round his head with his r hand.

DIAGRAM B

The Kolo leader by himself, or all the men dancers except the one next to the women, may perform lively steps with

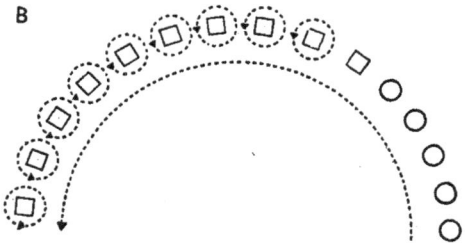

B

Leaping Turns to R and L, but not changing the rhythm of the dance; they may also use the Squatting Step.

DIAGRAMS C AND D

The men move into a procession with one of the Basic Steps. In formation, either as shown in Diagram C or in D, the men, except the ones nearest to the women, may perform the Leaping Turns or Squatting Steps. The women continue with the Basic Steps, which may develop into

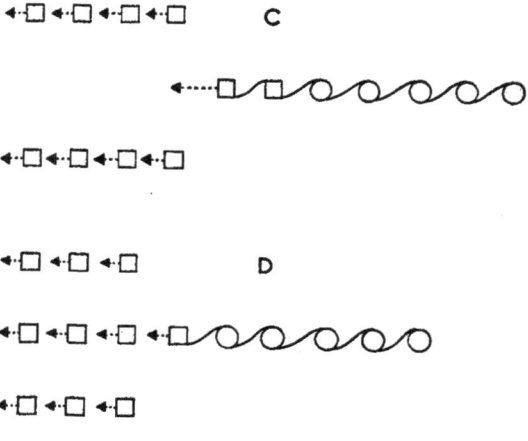

mple walking steps, while the procession is being formed.
The women remain in the chain throughout.

Dance: BASIC STEPS	MUSIC *Bars*
Body is turned to R when step is danced in chain.	
Step to R on r foot [*beat 1*].	1
Cross l foot in front of r, moving to R [*beat 2*].	
Repeat steps of bar 1.	2
Step to R on r foot, raising l foot [*beat 1*].	3
Hop on r foot [*beat 2*].	
Cross l foot in front of r foot, moving to R [*beat 1*].	4
Step to R on r foot [*beat 2*].	
Repeat steps of bar 4.	5
Cross l foot in front of r foot, moving to R [*beat 1*].	6
Close r foot to l foot, changing weight to r foot [*beat 2*].	
Cross l foot in front of r foot [*and*].	
The movements of these 6 bars may be repeated as often as the leader decides.	
The body is turned to R, as in Step 1.	
Step to R on r foot [*beat 1*].	1
Close l foot to r foot, changing weight [*beat 2*].	
Step to R on r foot [*and*].	
Cross l foot in front of r foot, moving to R [*beat 1*].	2
Close r foot to l foot [*beat 2*].	
Cross l foot in front of r foot, moving to R [*and*].	
Step to R on r foot, lifting l foot slightly [*beat 1*].	3

LAKA LISA

Macedonia: Skoplje region
Noted by Danica S. Janković
Arranged by Arnold Foster

Hold position [*beat 2*].	
Repeat the movements of Step 1, bars 4, 5 and 6.	4–6
The movements of these 6 bars may be repeated.	
3. The body is turned to R, as in Steps 1 and 2.	
Repeat the movements of Step 1, bars 1 and 2.	1–2
Step to R on r foot, lifting l foot slightly [*beat 1*].	3
Hold position [*beat 2*].	

Turn body square to front for the next 3 bars.	
Step backward on l foot [*beat 1*].	4
Step backward on r foot [*beat 2*].	
Step backward on l foot [*beat 1*].	5
Step forward on r foot [*beat 2*].	
Step forward on l foot [*beat 1*].	6
Close r foot to l foot without changing weight [*and*].	
Hold [*beat 2*].	

The movements of these 6 bars may be repeated.

STEPS FOR MEN DANCERS

The following steps may be danced by the Kolo leader or any of the men except those who remain beside the women. The steps may be used as described under Diagram B, or the men may move into a procession as shown in Diagrams C and D. In this case one of the Basic Steps is used (without any Cross steps) for the first three bars until the procession is formed, as unobtrusively as possible, and then the more acrobatic step begins on bar 4. 1-3

Leaping Turn

Step on l foot in place, turning half to L with a powerful body swing [*beat 1*]. 4
Step on r foot in place, turning half to L with body swing [*beat 2*].
Repeat turns on l and r feet. 5
Repeat turn on l foot [*beat 1*]. 6
Hop on l foot, turning half to L [*beat 2*].

This step may be repeated and may be danced turning to R, beginning on r foot.

Squatting Step

Squat quickly on both heels [*beat 1*]. 4
Straighten legs briskly and hop on l foot, stretching r leg obliquely forward [*beat 2*].
Repeat above, hopping on r foot on beat 2. 5
Repeat above, hopping on l foot on beat 2. 6

This step may be repeated as often as desired.

Each step may be danced to any part of the tune according to the will of the Kolo leader.

Plate 4   Macedonia: Skoplje region

BIBLIOGRAPHY

DJORDJEVIĆ, VIHOMIR R.—'Srpske Narodne Igre.' *Srpski Etnografski Zbornik*, Belgrade, vol. IX, 1907. (Serbian Folk Dances.)

DJORDJEVIĆ, VLADIMIR R.—*Srpske Igre za Violinu*. Belgrade, 1933. (Serbian Dance Tunes for the Violin.)

—— *Narodne Igre za Gudacki Orkestar*. Belgrade, 1934. (Folk-Dance Tunes for String Orchestra.)

JANKOVIĆ, DANICA S.—*Melodije Narodnih Igara*. Belgrade, 1937. (Folk-Dance Tunes. Supplement to *Narodne Igre*, vol. I, by L. and D. S. Janković.)

—— 'Russalia Dances.' *English Dance and Song*, vol. III, no. 5, May–June 1939.

—— 'Women's Dances in Yugoslavia.' (Translated by Fanny Foster.) *Countrywoman*, London, Sept. 1939.

JANKOVIĆ, LJUBICA and DANICA S.—*Narodne Igre*. 5 vòls. Belgrade, 1934, 1937, 1939, 1948, 1949. (National Dances.)

MAROLT, FRANCE.—*Slovenske Narodoslovne Študije*, vol. II: *Tri Obredja iz Bele Krajine*. Ljubljana, 1936. (Slovenian Folklore Studies: Three Rites from the White Krajina.)

FILM: *Igre Naroda Jugoslavije*. (Dances of the Peoples of Yugoslavia.) Jadran-Film, Zagreb, 1948. May be obtained through the Council for Science and Culture of the Yugoslav Government, Foreign Relations Department, Velikog Miloša Street 23, Belgrade; or through the Directorship of Information.

www.ingramcontent.com/pod-product-compliance
Lightning Source LLC
Chambersburg PA
CBHW042043280426
43661CB00093B/973